MW01109846

# Curv Your Dog

## and other hilarious cartoons

Curv Your Dog cartoons are the creation of Scott Bookner, a practicing pediatrician who lives in Scarsdale, New York. Dr. Bookner loves to make people laugh and has found his own little comedy niche in the form of cartoon drawing.

After drawing an occasional cartoon for a school newspaper or hospital newsletter, Dr. Bookner became much more engrossed in drawing in 1999. In March of 2000, with a great amount of help from his good friend, and computer wiz, Joon Kim, he launched www.CurvYourDog.com.

By 2003, www.CurvYourDog.com featured over 400 original cartoons by Dr. Bookner. The website has received tens of thousands of hits. After being urged by friends, family and patients (and driven by a human lust for fame and fortune), Dr. Bookner has finally decided to make 140 of his cartoons available in this book.

The ability to laugh and the ability to make others laugh are two of the greatest gifts we have. Enjoy the cartoons on the following pages. Some will make you smile. Hopefully, some will make you laugh out loud.

# Curv Your Dog

and other hilarious cartoons

_by_

_Scott Bookner_

A cataloguing record for this book that includes the U.S. Library of Congress Classification number, the Library of Congress Call number and the Dewey Decimal cataloguing code is available from the National Library of Canada. The complete cataloguing record can be obtained from the National Library's online database at: www.nlc-bnc.ca/amicus/index-e.html
ISBN 1-4120-2124-3

# TRAFFORD

**This book was published** *on-demand* **in cooperation with Trafford Publishing.**
On-demand publishing is a unique process and service of making a book available for retail sale to the public taking advantage of on-demand manufacturing and Internet marketing.
**On-demand publishing** includes promotions, retail sales, manufacturing, order fulfilment, accounting and collecting royalties on behalf of the author.

Suite 6E, 2333 Government St., Victoria, B.C. V8T 4P4, CANADA

| | | | |
|---|---|---|---|
| Phone | 250-383-6864 | Toll-free | 1-888-232-4444 (Canada & US) |
| Fax | 250-383-6804 | E-mail | sales@trafford.com |
| Web site | www.trafford.com | TRAFFORD PUBLISHING IS A DIVISION OF TRAFFORD HOLDINGS LTD. | |
| Trafford Catalogue #03-2672 | | www.trafford.com/robots/03-03-2672.html | |

10     9     8     7     6     5     4     3     2     1

*For Elissa, Ilana, Molly and Harrison*

# Acknowledgements

----------

I would like to acknowledge the following people who have made this work possible: Joon Kim, for his countless hours putting together and running www.CurvYourDog.com without ever asking for anything in return; Joseph Ferraro, my number one critic, for his many outstanding suggestions; Jennifer Henkind and Bonnie Zdanoff for their time spent reviewing every cartoon; Joel Zdanoff, who has the same warped sense of humor as me, and a number of whose cartoon ideas appear throughout this book; my mother, Arlene Bookner, who laughs at all of my cartoons, even when she doesn't get them; my dear departed father, Morton Bookner, who taught me to never stop pursuing my goals; my loving wife, Elissa, for supporting this project 100%, even though it seems at times that I am married to my computer; my three wonderful children, Ilana, Molly, and Harrison, who make every day a beautiful one; my many patients and their families, who make my other life's work worthwhile, and who have encouraged me to also continue my cartooning career; my favorite cartoonists who are Charles Schulz (*Peanuts*), Bill Watterson (*Calvin and Hobbes*), Berke Breathed (*Bloom County*), Bil Keane (*The Family Circus*), Mark Parisi (*Off the Mark*), and the greatest of them all: Gary Larson (*The Far Side*) who will always provide me with the Mt. Everest level of cartoon humor for which to strive.

# Contents

# Animals

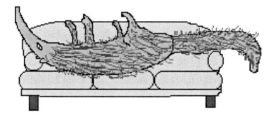

"I pronounce you: Spider and Wife.    You may now kill the husband."

"Great, great!  We'll do lunch on the 14th. Have your elephants call my elephants."

Stuffed animals

"It's from my brother. He's sorry he couldn't come, but he sends his egrets."

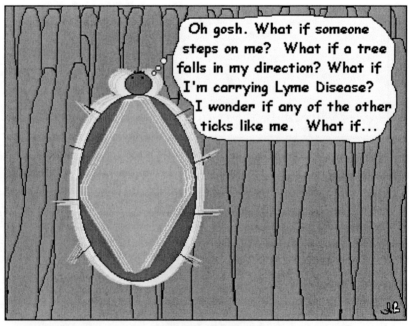

Nervous Tick

A lover of animals, Joanne did not believe in killing them for their fur.

"Well, I'll be! It's an alligator on a stalagmite! ..... or is that a crocodile on a stalactite?"

13

Although the Lion retained his figurehead position as "King," it was the Giraffe who now ruled, having been elected "Prime Minister of the Jungle."

# Outer Space

"That's one small step for Gligroborph; one giant leap for Gligroborphkind."

"That's why I told you kids to try to go before we left the house!"

Dexter and Harold snicker as Karl doesn't realize he has once again left the lens cap on.

"Ha! I wouldn't go out with you if you were the last glik on Xiglotron!"

Galileo loved to gaze into his lover's eyes.

"Earth in the side pocket."

# Computers

Before the Mouse, there was the Whale.

c.1982: The first e-mail

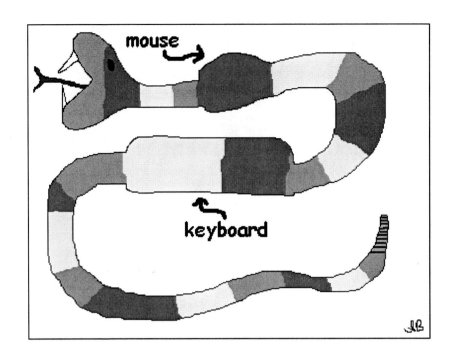

The Three Bears in the 21st Century.

# Broadway

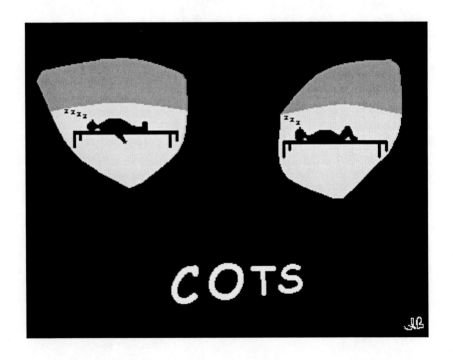

Artichokes on Broadway

Phantom of the Soap Opera

Surrey with the fridge on top

28

After the third mishap, the producers finally agreed to change the show to *"Fiddler* on the Roof."

Seventy-five trombones........ and one kazoo

# Monsters

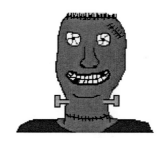

"Your cholesterol level is excellent, but I'm somewhat concerned about the amount of asbestos you've been eating."

Frankenstein's Half-brother

Nicknamed "Cheerful," Stan was not like the other Reapers.

If the Godfather had lived in Sleepy Hollow

Frankie Jr. gets caught with his hand in the cookie jar.

"Lady, I'd love to stay and talk, but I've got a plane to catch."

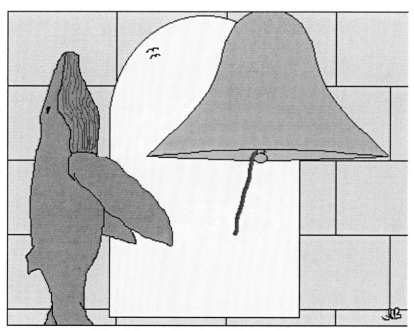

The Humpback of Notre Dame

"Good game today, Frankie. You da monster!"

# Driving

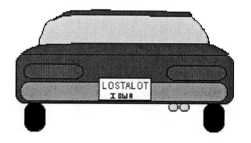

A Big Toe Truck

George's job is in serious jeopardy after losing the Florida Keys.

"Number 4, come in; Jenkins, do you read me? I'm telling you for the last time, get off the cell phone!"

**Cardinal Sin**

# Food

Cheese Gangsters.

"I was counting sheep and I got hungry."

**Peeking Duck**

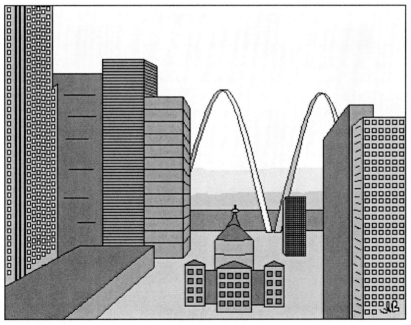

**St. McLouis**

45

There's a little-known farm in central California which produces most of the world's veggie-burgers.

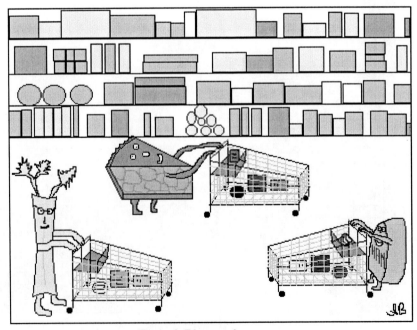

**Food Shopping**

46

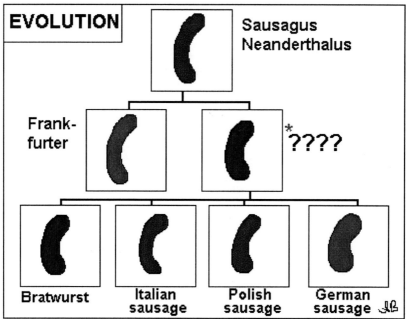

*Food scientists continue to search for the missing link.

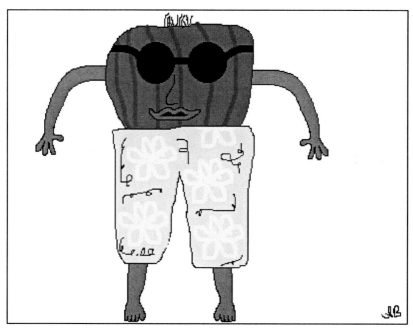

Bermuda Onion

"If you were not intending to murder your wife, then how do you explain that the police found this under your bed?"

# TV/Movies

**Planet of the Abes**

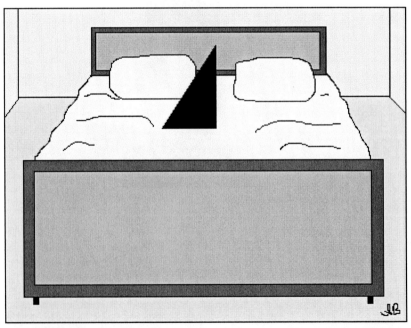

**Just when you thought it was safe to go back in the waterbed.....**

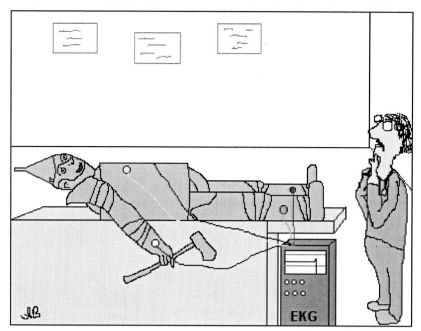

"Hmm.. That's strange. I could swear it's hooked up right, but I'm getting absolutely nothing."

The   Previously-Lone   Ranger

51

**Gorillas in the Midst**

**Scottish actor, Marlon Monroe**

Laurel & Harley

**Wet Butler**

# Children

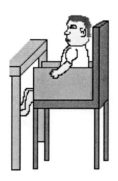

Transportation through the Ages

Mary had a little lamb.

"How is it I gave you a bath not twenty minutes ago, and already you've managed to get yourself clean again!?"

"How many times have I warned you about this?!"

The Farmer in the Deli

"Doctor, my baby has a bad cough and I was wondering if it's okay to take him outside."

# Sports

Tae Kwon Doe

Shaq dunks!

Sensing victory, Sean goes for the juggler.

Umpire State Building

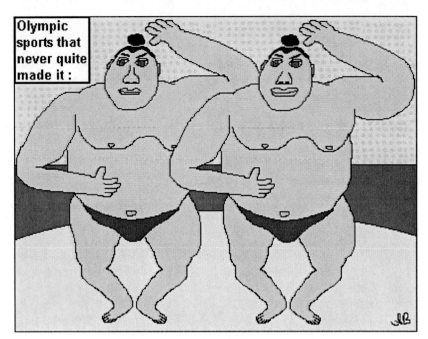

**Synchronized Sumo**

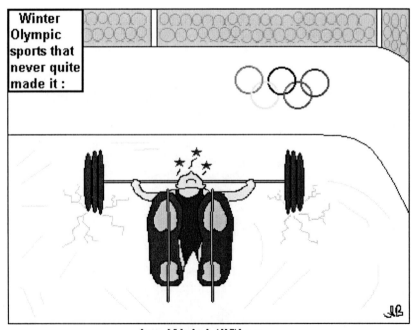

**Ice Weightlifting**

Shoeless Joe Jackson's Little League team

The ref whistles Harris for an illegal pick.

Baseball in Kansas: There's no base like Home.

# Medicine

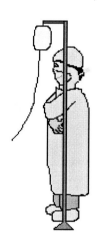

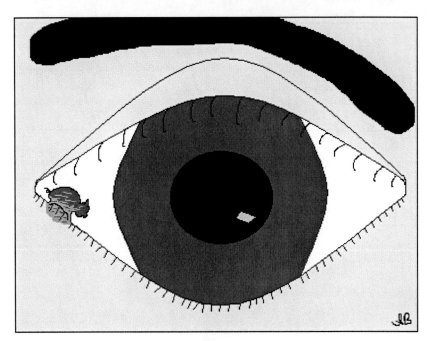

**Pig Stye**

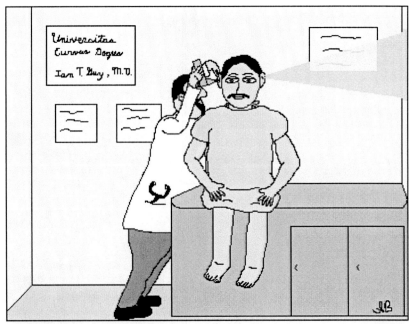

"Well, Mr. Anderson, the good news is that you don't have an ear infection...."

68

They say that José was not one to wear his heart on his sleeve; however, he did sometimes enjoy having his spleen on his lapel.

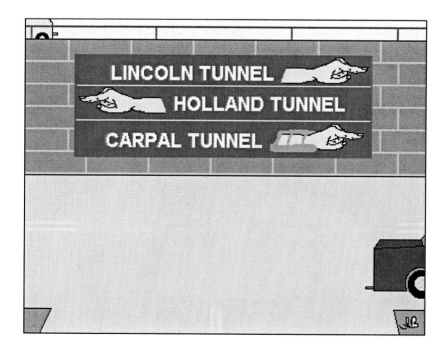

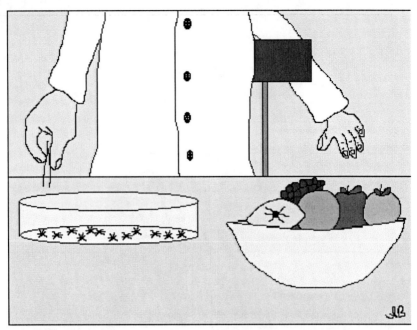

Unbeknownst to Professor Borrelli, one of his ticks has escaped and is about to start an epidemic of Lemon & Lyme Disease.

Pat has a cute appendicitis.

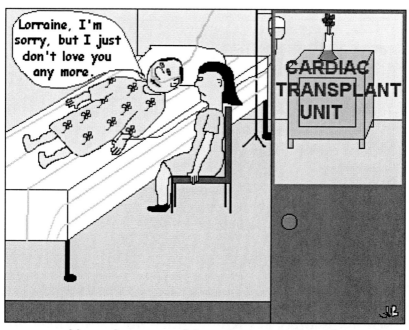

Harry has a sudden change of heart.

At the Appendix Family reunion ...

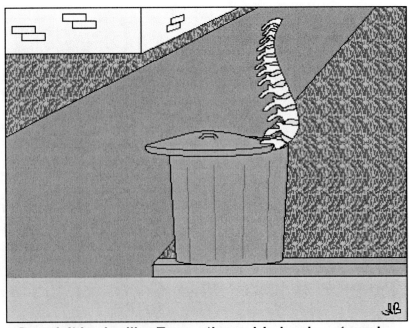

Oops! It looks like Roger threw his back out again.

# Art

Picasso makes improvements to the Mona Lisa.

The Next-to-Last Supper

Qué Seurat, Seurat

When Jackson Pollock was 18 months old

**Dan Quayle commissions Andy Warhol**

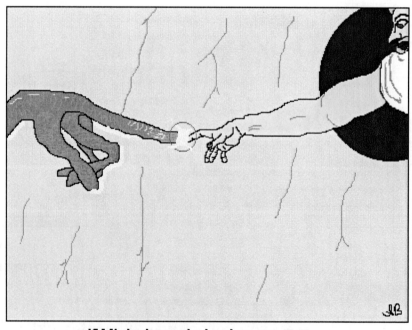

**If Michelangelo had seen *E.T.***

The girls just melted when Mr. Dali was around.

Escher's bathroom

**Whistler's Mother turns on Maxell.**

# Music

Hank and Doreen were having second thoughts about wanting a home where the buffalo roam and the deer and the antelope play.

The Silicon Valley Orchestra is led by Giulio Lambini,
one of the world's greatest semi-conductors.

The Beastie Babies

The Ungrateful Dead

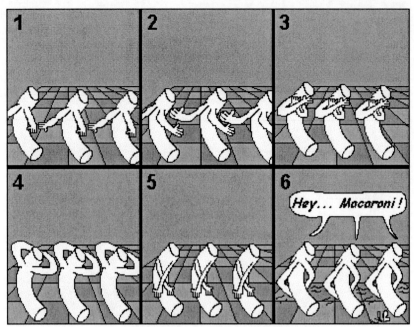

How to dance *The Macaroni*

# New Products

You've got mail!
Open mail now?
Yes ⊙   No

Introducing the Dumbrella

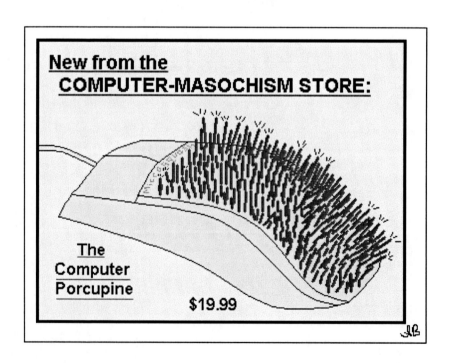

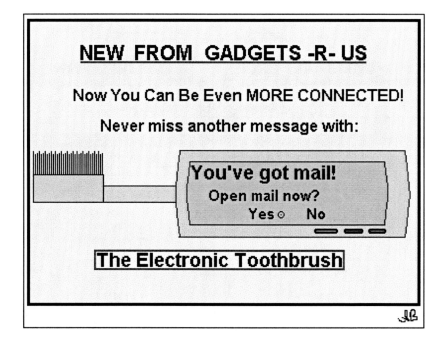

# History

Billy the Kidder

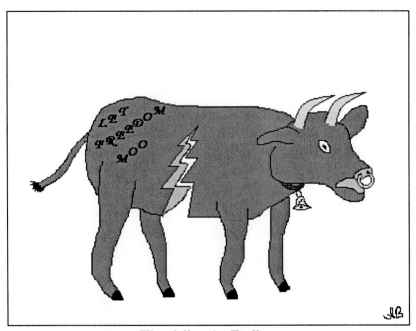

The Liberty Bull

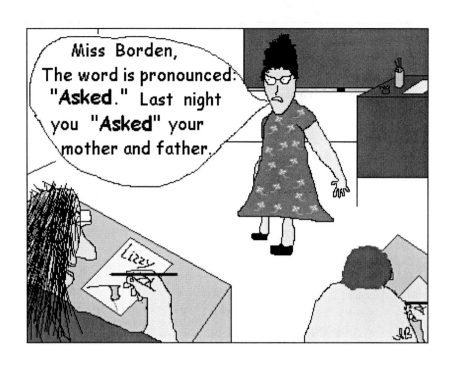

Joan of Arkansas

Cajun night in ancient Rome

Debate over the Right to Bare Arms

Edward Bulwer Lytton finds out the hard way that
he was incorrect regarding the pen versus the sword.

# Miscellaneous

"Joanne, will you look at the size of the rock on her!"

Although he was an intelligent and successful bank - owner, Emil still had trouble figuring out how to get the clock to stop flashing 12:00.

Sleeping Beauty meets Rip Van Winkle.

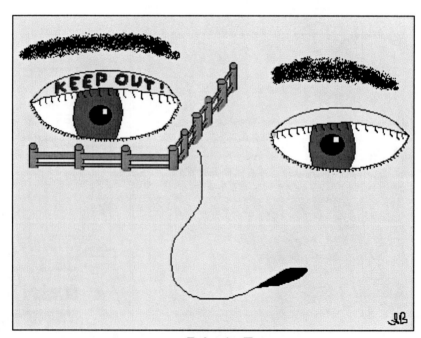

Private Eye

At the home of the invisible man and woman

When editers miss things.

ISBN 141202124-3

9 781412 021241